PREPARING YOUR OWN CV

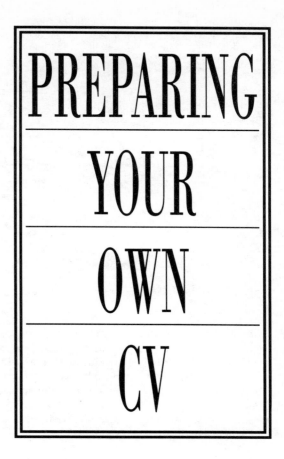

PREPARING YOUR OWN CV

HOW TO IMPROVE YOUR CHANCES OF GETTING THE JOB YOU WANT

Second Edition

Rebecca Corfield

KOGAN PAGE

For YB

First published in 1990
Reprinted 1991, 1992, 1993, 1994, 1995 (twice), 1996, 1997 (twice)
Second edition 1999

Kogan Page Limited
120 Pentonville Road
London N1 9JN

© Rebecca Corfield, 1990, 1999

British Library Cataloguing in Publication Data
A CIP record for this book is available from the British Library.
ISBN 0 7494 2852 X

Typeset by Saxon Graphics Ltd, Derby
Printed and bound in Great Britain by Clays Ltd, St Ives plc

Contents

Contents

Introduction

The world of work is changing fast. Jobs are more temporary and insecure. As a result, most of us will change careers and move in and out of different jobs many times in our working lives, perhaps going on training courses in-between to make ourselves more employable.

This means that applying for jobs is becoming a much more frequent activity in an increasingly competitive environment. The way we present ourselves is crucial to being successful in the job market.

The fact that you are reading this book is likely to mean that you are either:

- looking for a job
- trying to change your job for some reason
- planning for a future change of career
- preparing your personal job-search materials
- advising people in one of the above situations.

You know that the key to getting an interview rests on impressing an employer in writing. You have heard that a curriculum vitae or CV may help you to get the job of your choice and need help knowing where to start.

The importance of a good CV

Feeling that you are in the wrong career or cannot get the job of your choice can be very depressing. Finding a job, or a better job, is fraught with difficulties at the best of times, and having to try and present yourself in a positive light when you are probably feeling demoralised and not at your most self-confident may seem too challenging. But with the right help you will be able to compile a CV which will give you a big advantage in overcoming this hurdle.

Anything which aids you in your search is valuable, but a good CV can be a real boon. A curriculum vitae is extremely versatile and can enhance your job prospects, regardless of your circumstances. You will benefit from compiling a curriculum vitae, whether you have:

- many qualifications or none
- done too many jobs, or never worked
- been unemployed for long periods
- had career success or have not yet found your niche
- excellent references or none.

When an employer is looking for an employee, one of the applicants has to be successful. That person could be you – if your CV stands out from the rest as being full of evidence that you are the best candidate for the job. Equally important, if this evidence is presented in a concise and attractive way, your CV can be a powerful influence working for you.

Employers want an easy time when they are looking for suitable candidates to employ. If they can spot a good potential employee from the papers that arrive in response to an advert, they will spend much less time than usual in finding the right person for the job.

How to get the most out of this book

This book is written to guide you in the first steps towards putting together a curriculum vitae or CV for yourself – even if you have never heard the words before. You do not need to be an expert at getting jobs, a 'high-flier' or someone who is good at 'selling yourself'. The curriculum vitae will do that for you.

Having the right CV is just part of the larger operation of finding a job – and that can be like playing a game. Several factors can help you to win in this game, and having a nicely written and presented curriculum vitae is the place to start. Employers know roughly what type of person they are looking for, and you have to:

(a) try to work out what they want, and then

(b) convince them that you fit that description and are the candidate with the most to offer.

These advertisements are typical of those seen every day. Increasingly, as well as in Jobcentres, employment agencies and newspapers, job vacancies can be found on the World Wide Web.

We offer a competitive salary, an enjoyable work environment, and benefits such as company discounts, concert tickets, and contributory pension scheme.

Please write with career details to

Margaret Smith
Recruitment & Training Officer
VP UK Limited
1 Oxford Street
London W1V 6HE

PA-GROUP OFFICE ADMINISTRATOR
based in PETERBOROUGH

We are the international headquarters for a new market-driven company, involved in the development and distribution of highly innovative home products.

The job: PA to our Chief Executive with UK and international responsibilities.

You are: Articulate and practical. You have excellent keyboard and other secretarial skills. You have good communication skills and can be part of a happy, ambitious team.

We offer: An excellent starting salary (£25,500, pension, medical insurance and generous performance bonus).

Please send your CV to: Mr Marcus Smith, Group Operations Manager, Aspen Lifestyle Products Ltd, Aspen House, Horsefair, Porterham PE1 5BQ.

To apply for vacancies like these you need to have your own impressive CV at the ready.

Once you have read through this book and used the practical advice to compile your own CV, you will have started to take more control over your role in job hunting, and the next steps will not seem so difficult.

Chapter 1 will explain what a CV is, and show what a standard layout looks like. In Chapter 2 we shall cover how to put the document to the best use. We shall study the content of a good CV in Chapter 3, and then examine how it should be presented for maximum impact in Chapter 4.

In Chapter 5, you can look at real examples of other people's documents and learn from their best efforts before you start on your own. There are certain things that you should *not* do in a CV, and these are explained later in the book. The final chapter draws together all the information and gives you a step-by-step guide to compiling your own effective curriculum vitae.

CHAPTER 1
What is a CV?

A CV is an outline on paper, of a person's educational and professional history. This may sound as though it should only be used by 'professionals' or those with high-level qualifications, but *everyone* can benefit from having a well-written and well-presented CV when job hunting. It is a simple and accessible way of introducing yourself to potential employers and can be a vital tool in obtaining the chance to impress them face-to-face at an interview.

What does a CV look like?

Every CV will look different, and that is the way it should be. Like the real 'story of your life', it will be different from every other person's story, for each of us is unique.

What does curriculum vitae mean?

The words come from the Latin and mean literally 'the course of your life' or the brief story of your career. The term is often abbreviated to CV, and these two letters are used to represent the term in this book.

Therefore there is no such thing as the *right* way to construct a CV. Every careers adviser has different ideas about the best way to design and fill the document. Each thinks that this or that should be included, in this or that manner. This book outlines the way I expect employers will be most impressed, and uses three simple rules that you will find repeated throughout the book:

1. Keep it simple.

2. Make it clear.

3. Keep it short.

In fact these rules should be applied to any written document.

What is in a CV?

Standard CVs are usually split into a maximum of seven different sections:

1. *Personal details:*
   Includes name, address, telephone number, date of birth, nationality, etc.

2. *Education:*
   Provides dates, names and locations of schools and colleges attended and details of any qualifications that you may have obtained.

3. *Employment:*
   Specifies dates, employers' names and locations, job title and main activities/achievements of each position held.

4. *Other skills:*
   Covers your other practical abilities or skills.

5. *Interests:*
   Includes hobbies, sport and leisure activities.

6. *Additional information:*
   Details other skills or type of work wanted.

7. *References:*
   Names and addresses of two people who will provide character references for you.

How do you start to write a CV?

Writing a CV for yourself is time-consuming and laborious, but certainly worth the effort. The way to start is to read through this short book in order to understand the basics of compiling a CV. Then you can begin working through your own career history, guided by the examples contained in the book.

It would be much simpler if there were CVs in this book that you could just copy, but unfortunately, because each person has different experiences and skills, your CV *has* to be completely original, and unique to you alone.

Obviously, you can learn from other people and on pages 44–72 in Chapter 5 you will find many different examples of the way that CVs look once they have been put together. At the end of the book on pages 81–82 in Chapter 6, a blank form has been included for you to use when you start compiling a version for yourself.

The finished product will aim to:

● highlight the good points of your experience and skills

● play down any weaknesses in your history.

How long should a CV be?

Most CVs should be limited to just two sheets of A4 paper, so this document will not take you too long to write, once you know where to start and have help in presenting the information correctly.

When your CV is finished you will be able to update it regularly as you add to your experience and skills. The effort will be worth while and your confidence in presenting yourself to potential employers will grow when you see how impressive your history can look, once it has been well thought out and displayed.

CHAPTER 2

What is a CV used for?

A CV can be used for many different purposes:

- applying for advertised vacancies when the employer specifies that applicants must send in a CV – see the examples on pages 44–72.

- applying for vacancies in a speculative manner, or 'on spec'. This is when you write off to companies in the hope that they may have vacancies, now or in the future. If there are no current vacancies you can ask them to keep your name on file. Your CV can be a lasting record of your details for the company to refer to in case of employment opportunities in the future. You can find companies' names and addresses in newspapers, trade and telephone directories or on the World Wide Web.

- by employment agencies or Jobcentres when they are putting your name forward to the employers on their books.

- as an *aide-mémoire*, or memory-jogger, when you are completing application forms. All the information about your history will be included in this document, and this will save you from having to remember all the dates and information each time you have a different form to fill in.

- for general business purposes, when self-employed or doing consultancy work, etc.

- as an introduction to companies or banks when you need to explain your background for some purpose.

- when making an application to a college for a course of study or training.

How can a CV enhance your job prospects?

Have you ever seen a job that looked interesting, but have not applied for it because it asked you to send in your CV and you did not have one prepared? This situation need never arise again.

Many jobs that are advertised in newspapers are filled very quickly indeed. If you can rush your CV to the company concerned, your application stands as good a chance as that of anyone else. However, if you are really keen on a job, it is no good dashing off a CV at the last minute. Hasty work will not match up to the best of the competition. An impressive CV needs time and care to compile.

Be prepared

Once you have produced a CV that you are pleased with, you have one big advantage over many other job-seekers: you are ready to apply for a job whenever a suitable one comes up. Instead of flying into a panic at the thought of having to prepare all your details, you will be ready to send off your personal introduction to the employer promptly.

Another great advantage of having an impressive CV to hand is that the same information can be sent to any number of different employers; the only information you need to change is the covering letter that is sent with it. Your CV will be deliberately designed to be suitable for many different situations.

How do you start to compile an effective CV?

Working on a CV that you are really proud of can take a long time. The finished document can be improved on and altered continually, even when you are ready to use it.

Making sure that you are including the right information is a time-consuming business initially. All your details need to be listed, and then you must be ruthless in weeding out any unnecessary information. A short CV is the only one that will be read.

The importance of presentation

Once you are happy with the content, the correct presentation of the document can be as challenging a task. A good CV will speak volumes about the sort of person you are. If you have taken the time to sort out the document properly, you will appear well organised and thorough (useful in any job), and if the CV is well presented, you will look as though you are a person who is careful about details and confident at the same time.

To start with, you will need to spend time collating the details of all the jobs you have done in the past, as well as the facts of your educational career. This may mean rooting around in old diaries or records and asking family members for their help. Certificates from school or college can provide useful education details and pay slips may tell you about the dates of jobs. You may not want to include all this in the final version, but collecting everything together enables you to make clearer choices about what to keep in. One important point to bear in mind is that you want to be able to use the finished CV for more than one application, on more than one occasion.

A CV is never used on its own, and will always be accompanied by a covering letter (see the example at the end of Chapter 6 on page 80). This letter is your opportunity to be specific about exactly how you fit the particular job that you are applying for, picking out the relevant skills, qualifications or experience that you have detailed in your CV.

Stressing your good points

Writing the CV is excellent practice in being assertive about yourself and your achievements. Most people are hopelessly bad at putting their best points forward. We are all more used to being shy and quiet about our assets. But each of us is unique and has our own history, strengths and ambitions, and those that relate to you can shine out from your completed CV.

Job applications require you to be positive about everything you have been through so far, whether it be many different jobs, all for a short period, or bringing up children away from the paid work market.

Minimising your weaknesses

Sometimes there will be aspects of your career history that you are not happy about. Although it would be wrong to be untruthful about your details, there are ways of accenting those things which you *are* proud of, to take the attention away from anything else. This means that you maximise your achievements and minimise the rest. As we work through the different sections of the CV in the next chapter, looking at what information to include, we will consider ways of handling problem cases.

CHAPTER 3
The content of your CV

What should be included?

So how do you start to put together your own CV? This chapter looks at *what* information to use, and Chapter 4 contains advice about *how* to present the information in the best way.

What you put into your CV is crucial to the way that it is perceived by the reader. In Chapter 2, the main sections of a CV were explained. Now we will consider all the sections in turn in order to see what should and should not be included in each.

Remember the three important points mentioned in Chapter 1:

- Keep it simple.
- Make it clear.
- Keep it short.

Although there is no single right way to compile a CV, this is one method of getting a good CV for yourself.

Making your CV stand out

At the stage when your CV arrives on the employer's desk, he or she knows nothing more about you than the information that you are going to reveal in your CV. This means that you have a responsibility to do yourself justice, by explaining easily and simply who you are, and what you have done so far. You are an interesting and valuable person and your CV is the means by which you convey this to an employer.

The one way to ensure that your CV is noticed by an employer is to make it very obvious if you have done anything at all unusual. If you have travelled on a school or college trip, been involved with any voluntary groups or in different sporting activities, make sure you include these points.

You may be noticed by the employer just because there is something different about your CV which makes it stand out from all the others. If you can describe some activity that other people will not have taken part in, you will appear to have had different experiences from those of others, and therefore, to an employer, you may be more worth employing.

At this stage, all we are trying to do is to find out what material *could* be put into your CV. The amount of information that you compile may well end up being cut down a great deal, but that stage will come later on in this book.

Let us look at the CV for Patricia Mary Sharp, as an example:

1. Personal details
This section is usually not too difficult to compile, as it is just about the factual details of your life. Name, address and telephone number are put at the beginning of the CV so that your name and the way to contact you cannot be overlooked. This means that it would be easy for an interested employer to get in touch with you.

Name:
Names are written as:

Patricia SHARP.

Middle names are unnecessary as they will only confuse the reader. The surname (or family name) should come at the end. This order of names makes more sense than Sharp

Patricia, as this is not the way her name is normally used. We do not use P M Sharp either, as initials will also be difficult for an employer to understand and remember.

If you have more than one name (for instance married women who also use their maiden name), make sure you use the name that you would want to be called if you were employed as a result of the CV.

As some names can be unusual, it helps to put your second (or family name) in capital letters, so that it can be easily identified.

Address:
Always use your full address and postcode.

Telephone number:
Always include your telephone number if you have one. An interested employer may just want to pick up the phone in order to talk to you. If you are not on the telephone, try to find a friend or relative whose number you could use, so that messages could be taken on your behalf – as long as you are sure that they will be taken reliably. Only use a work number if it really does not matter if you are called at work.

Put the full STD code and number, eg:

0171 928 0000 *or* Oxford (01865) 000000

to be as clear as possible.

Electronic mail:
Include your e-mail address if you have one.

Date of birth:
15 July 1973 looks clearer than 15.07.73 or 15/7/73.

Use your date of birth rather than putting your age. If you write 37 this year, you will have to update it to 38 once your birthday arrives, and so on every year. If you feel that you are either particularly young or mature in age, do not be tempted to omit your date of birth. Employers are genuinely interested in your age, and there will be an opportunity under section 6, 'Additional Information', to add more details about yourself and to put your age in a positive light.

Nationality:
For some jobs, this aspect of your personal details is very important. If you are from another country, it is essential for you to specify that you are able to work here, eg:

Nigerian (with full UK work permit).

Refugee status is also worth mentioning, eg:

Ethiopian (with refugee status in the UK).

On the basis of keeping the information as simple as possible, some personal details which are not worth including are:

height, weight, place of birth, country of birth

unless you have reason to think that including one of these factors in your CV would increase your chances of getting the job. For instance, if you were born in the place where the company is based, or if the job particularly requires a certain physical standard.

Some people include a recent head-and-shoulders photograph with their CV. I think that this can attract interest to your CV and get you noticed, particularly where physical appearance is relevant to the job, but the practice is still uncommon.

2. Education
This section is for you to outline your educational history from secondary school onwards. The further away this time is from the present, the less relevant the information will be. So, for instance, school leavers will give full details of all the subjects they studied in this section, as they will have less, or perhaps

no information to put in the employment history section. More information on presenting a CV for a school leaver is included with the example on pages 45–47 in Chapter 5.

The information needed is, first, the dates that you attended your secondary school (from age 11 onwards) – either just the years, or the months and years. Next, the name and location of the school(s) should be included, although the whole address is not necessary. To locate a school, just the town and county or the city and postcode are appropriate. The last pieces of information are any examinations passed or, if none were taken, the subjects studied. You do not need to put down subjects in which you failed an exam – our intention is to stress strengths and minimise weaknesses. If you obtained distinctions, prizes or scholarships in certain subjects, include this information as it will set you apart from other candidates.

College details should be given in the same way. To use our example again, Patricia Sharp includes the following information:

| 1983–
1988 | Swansmead School
Birmingham B14 | **GCSEs:**
English language
Mathematics, History
Science, CDT |
| 1988–
1990 | Bishops Technical College
Wolverhampton | **BTEC National Diploma:**
Business Studies |

As you can see from this example, school experience is usually put in chronological order, with your first school coming at the top of the list and then other periods of study listed in order, finishing with the most recent.

3. Employment
This section covers the different jobs that you have done. The information required is very similar to the last section on your educational details. You need to research all the starting and

finishing dates of all the different jobs you have done, including part-time, vacation and voluntary jobs especially if you have not had much employment experience.

Either just the year, or the month and year, is again appropriate for each position. If you are older and have had many jobs, or have had gaps between jobs that you would like to 'smooth over', then just the year may be appropriate.

For this section, the order of your employment history is reversed. Starting with your most recent job, you list them all and end up with your first employment. The reason for this is so that the job in which you had the most responsibility, normally your last, comes first.

1987– 1990	Perkins Confectioners London SW15	**Clerical Assistant:** Word-processing, invoicing, dealing with customers, filing, telephone work, keeping petty cash.

The main difference between this section and the last is that here we need to say what the job title was in each case, and to specify the main duties for each different job.

You can see that only the main duties are listed, and they are written in note form. Also, they all begin with a verb: word-processing, invoicing, dealing with, filing, keeping, etc. To write full sentences would take up too much room.

If the type of employment is not clear from the name of the company, and it is relevant to the job that you did, it is worth putting it in brackets after the name, eg:

Simpkins **Clerk:**
(Solicitors)

Before you start to write up your own details, try to think of all the things that you did in each job, and list them all. Even though it may seem obvious to you that a clerical assistant would do some filing, it may not be clear to anyone who has not done exactly the same job before, and it may be just what the employer is looking for evidence of.

The idea of a CV is that your history will be seen in date order. Remember, if you have had many large gaps in your employment history, you may find it more useful to put just the year of starting and finishing a job so that the end of each job merges more into the beginning of the next.

If you were in charge of other people in a job, make sure that you mention this at the beginning of your duties, and also include any promotions that you received during your time in the job.

If you have had many different jobs, remember that the important fact is what sort of person you are now, and what skills and experience you have acquired to date. Jobs from further back may show your breadth of experience, but in that case they can be grouped together, such as:

'I have worked in many different types of employment during vacations, including shop, office and factory work'

or:

'I have four years of pay-roll and accounts work with agencies throughout the Birmingham area.'

I do not recommend including details either about why you left each job, or about what salary/wages you earned in each position. If the employer wishes to find out these things, they can be discussed in a subsequent interview.

4. Other skills
Include in this section any other skills that you have learnt that you would like an employer to know about. Examples could be familiarity with computer packages such as word processing or spreadsheets; first aid; full, clean driving licence; basic or advanced language ability.

5. Interests

Your interests can help to show that you have a well-rounded personality and do not live for work alone. Any interests that you have or have had in the past which are out of the ordinary will help you to stand out.

I would not recommend being too specific about any political or religious interests unless they are of direct relevance to the position that you are applying for. To make sure that you do not prejudice your chances, it is better to say that you are actively involved in the local community – the reader of your CV may hold different views from your own.

Try to put down some physical activities, as well as some cultural ones, to show that you are a healthy, active and lively person. Note form is all that is needed here, eg:

> Swimming, karate, walking, travel, reading, cinema and cookery.

You do not actually have to spend time on *all* these activities at the moment, but be sure that you know enough to talk about every interest you list at the interview. Employers often pick on your hobbies as an easy area of questioning. In this example, they may want to know what style of karate you studied. Not an easy question to answer if the nearest you ever got to karate was watching a Bruce Lee film, and the employer is a black belt!

If you belong to any clubs, societies or professional bodies, you can mention them here. Remember that an employer will be interested in any activity that makes yours stand out from the crowd of CVs that he or she is considering.

When making the decision about what information to include in this section, always remember that the point of putting down your hobbies is to show the reader that you are a well-rounded and balanced person, with a satisfactory life of your own outside work.

Try to avoid the most obvious interests, which we all share. This means that 'reading, socialising and watching TV' should be avoided.

6. Additional information

With many CVs to consider, employers are looking for more than just the minimum skills and experience necessary to be able to do the job. They want people who will fit in the company or organisation properly. Therefore to get to the next stage of the recruitment process and be invited to an interview, your CV must also describe the sort of person you are. After all, you and I could have attended the same school or college and worked in the same places but we would still be completely different people.

To find material to use in this section, write a list of ten words or short phrases that describe your good points. The words in the list may be those that have been used about you in references or appraisals in the past, or compliments that have been paid to you when you have made a valuable contribution at work. They should describe some aspect of your personality rather than things you know how to do. The idea is to gather positive words that help portray your character at its best. Some words apply to just about all of us, so try not to include very obvious ones such as 'punctual', 'friendly' or 'sociable' in your ten.

Here is one list as an illustration.

- motivated;
- calm;
- polite;
- loyal;
- thorough;
- hardworking;
- serious-minded;
- accurate;
- determined and a good team worker.

Once you have compiled your list, pick the six or seven most relevant to the kind of job you are likely to apply for. For each of the words or phrases, construct a sentence about yourself, where possible giving an example of when you have demonstrated that kind of behaviour and in this way work up a short passage about your personality.

From the list above, the result follows:

'I am a hardworking and loyal person. My experience working in shops has taught me that a polite and calm approach to caring for the customer works best. I try always to be accurate in my work and take a pride in being thorough about details. I enjoy working as part of a team.'

Here is the list of a completely different character: 'Energetic; determined; keen to win; persuasive; ambitious; talkative; good sense of humour; creative; hardworking; quick learner.'

The resulting paragraph from this list could be:

'My sales training built on my persuasive skills and natural determination. I learn quickly and my good sense of humour helps in any team when deadlines approach. I try to be creative in any task and work hard to contribute with energy and ambition to agreed team goals.'

Now compose your own list and paragraph. The result may sound as though you are blowing your own trumpet too much but please resist the temptation to include negative points or to qualify what you write as in 'fairly good', 'quite accurate' or 'usually hardworking'. Plain, positive words are needed here to allow your strengths to shine out of your CV. All other job applicants will be portraying themselves in the best light possible, so do not hold back. This section is normally written out in full sentences.

This section can be very important for those with gaps in the other sections of their CV. For instance, if you have brought up children and have therefore been out of paid work for some time, this is the place to explain the gap in your career. An example of this type of CV is included in Chapter 5, on pages 59–61.

If you have travelled for a time, you can write about it here. If you are changing career direction, this section is your chance to explain why you are interested in the new type of work.

Here are several examples of the type of information that could be included.

'For the last seven years I have been looking after my two children. This experience, coupled with my previous job, has taught me how to budget and plan, keep to deadlines, organise work schedules, work as part of a team and delegate tasks.'

'I am mature, very adaptable and can work cheerfully under pressure. I am painstaking in my work, honest, punctual and trustworthy. I make friends easily and enjoy working as part of a team.'

'I have many years' experience as a finisher in the clothing industry. After bringing up my family, I am eager to return to full-time employment and use my expert skills to contribute to an effective team. I can offer reliability, punctuality, stability and commitment.'

'During the past few years, I have spent a lot of time doing voluntary work in the community, both here and abroad, helping to provide for the needs of others.'

'I have extensive experience in designing, writing and testing programs, and versatile knowledge of software and operating systems.'

7. References
You should name here two people who can be approached to provide a reference for you. One should be your last employer or someone from your last school or college, and the other should be a friend. The reference from your last employer can just be given as the Personnel Department of a large firm, if there is no particular person to write it for you.

The reason for references is so that the reader can see that you have referees who are prepared to vouch for your competence and character. They will often be contacted, so you must make sure that you ask their permission first.

If you are sending your CV out to many addresses, make sure that your referees are happy about being contacted by a variety of people over a long period. You cannot afford to have an employer contact someone whose name you have given as a referee, only to be told that he or she does not want to vouch for you.

Character referees should normally have a good job of their own, and must not be in your own family, although if a family member has a different name from yours (such as an in-law), nobody would know that you were related. Family doctors or priests can often be prevailed upon to act as referees if they have known you for some time, but again you must get their permission first.

Include a telephone number for both references if possible, as the employer may well just decide to pick up the telephone on the spur of the moment. Before you give out home telephone numbers, check that this is acceptable to your referees. If you are applying for various vacancies it can be helpful to discuss the nature of each particular job with your referees to help them target the information they provide to the prospective employer.

Please remember that anyone who is prepared to write a reference for you is doing you a big favour. Regular appreciation makes sure all your referees feel properly valued by you.

If you have recently arrived in this country or have been travelling, and only have references from another country, I strongly advise you to contact the referees and get them to write an open letter or testimonial on your behalf. This can be used each time you send off your CV: send a photocopy (never send the original) of the letter, attached to the back of your CV.

The reason for this is that many employers are put off by the fact that it will take them a number of weeks to get a reference for you, but if they can see the testimonial in front of them, it may not prejudice them against you. In this case, only your two references are needed. Do not be tempted to include lots of photocopies of testimonials or exam certificates, as great wodges of paper will just put the employer off.

Problems

'I was sacked from my last job, and I know they will give me a bad reference.'

This can be overcome by using an earlier employer for the reference, and explaining why in an interview. You can say that you experienced personal difficulties in your last employment. You will have to rehearse your description of the events exactly, before any interview, to make sure that you can sound convincing.

If you have only had one job and been sacked, you will have to try and put the situation in the best light possible to explain what happened. Use two personal references on your CV. Perhaps you could do some voluntary work to give yourself another reference – even if only for a short time.

'I can get an excellent reference from my last employer, but she spends long periods out of the country. Should I still include her as one of my referees?'

Anything that is likely to put a prospective employer off is a bad idea. If the employer is interested in taking you on, he or she will not want to wait for six months before receiving your reference. I would advise you to find a substitute referee who can guarantee a quick response to any enquiries. Another alternative is to get an open testimonial from this woman explaining that she is often unavailable, which you could then include with your CV.

CHAPTER 4

Presentation

You can now collect together all the material that you need to put into your CV. The way that you present the CV is of the utmost importance. You know that when you buy goods, you are often attracted by the packaging on the outside as much as by what is inside. The same is true of the CV. Giving employers your notes to read would leave them scratching their heads in confusion about what it all means, and they would probably not be very impressed.

After all, that is the whole point of compiling a CV in the first place. You want to present yourself in the best possible light to employers, and the way that they will judge you is by the impression they gain from those two sheets of A4 paper. For that is the only information they have to go on. Everything in this chapter is to further that aim.

When thinking about presenting your CV in the best way try to avoid anything that might put an employer off. This means that the CV must look:

- plain
- attractive
- easy to read.

Written, typed or word-processed?

If at all possible, get your CV done on a word-processor, even if you have to pay for the privilege. It will come out typed, can be edited with ease, and has the great advantage of being easily updated at any time in the future.

Do not attempt to word-process your own document if you have never used a computer before and cannot type. It will take you ages and you will probably make many mistakes as well. You can pay to have your CV typed by somebody else, but shop around before you pay out a lot of money, to make sure that you get the best deal possible.

These days, many people have word-processors at home, and you may be able to find a friend who will help you to get it done. The great advantages of word-processors are that you can make any corrections easily and you can run off as many copies as you like, whenever you want them.

The second best alternative is to have your CV typed. It looks smart and professional but will have to be completely re-typed if any of your details change. Never be tempted to use correction fluid to make changes to your CV, or to add information using a different typewriter, as it will look messy.

If it is at all possible, have your CV word-processed or typed up. Your local Jobcentre may be able to find a place to get this done if you are not working and need help with this task.

Order

The order of the different sections recommended in this book has been tried and tested many times. The simplicity of the design seems to impress and interest employers. If you start your CV with a paragraph about your skills and talents, the employer may well be impressed, but will soon forget who you are.

The beauty of this standard layout is that the contents follow a logical pattern. First you are introducing yourself, then saying where you have come from, in terms of your education and employment experience. You then go on to explain your other skills and any other relevant information, including your interests and referees. You are telling the complete story.

Length

Your CV should not take up more than two sheets of A4 paper using one side only. Some people have difficulty in stretching their CVs past one side, particularly if they have little experience of work. Often a CV will stretch over four or five sides of A4 at the first draft. Let us look at each of these problems in turn.

Problems
'My CV is too short.'

If you have just left school it will be necessary to make your CV more of a personal information sheet. This gives you much more scope for including information about other activities that you have taken part in at school or college. For instance, you can describe your role in teams that you have played in or groups that you joined. See the example on page 45 of Chapter 5.

If you took GCSEs at school you should be able to include your record of achievement, which charts your progress through the fourth and fifth years. You may wish to have one sheet of personal information with your record of achievement attached, or you could use the record to give you more details for your CV.

'My CV is too long.'

You must reduce the length of your CV to two sides if possible. Nobody reads more than two sides. Imagine you are a busy personnel officer desperately trying to check through the pile of CVs on your desk. With 20 to read in half an hour, you would find any excuse to reduce the pile by one.

The exceptions to this rule are older graduates who may have many college courses and jobs to fit in or those who have had many different jobs over a long time period. On no account should *any* CV be longer than three sides of A4 paper.

'My CV covers more than one side of A4, but only reaches half way down the second.'

Stretch the whole document out (easy on a word-processor) until it covers the two sides easily. In other words, add more space around your name, to help it stand out, and make bigger gaps between the different sections. Place the referees one beneath the other instead of next to each other. The more white space showing on the CV, the easier it will be to read.

'I now have six pages of rough draft for my CV. How will it all fit on to two sides of A4?'

Be ruthless! Remember – keep it simple, make it clear, keep it short. Use brief phrases, in note form, for the details of your education and employment experience. Edit your work to the bone, even if that means drafting the CV four or five times more. Make it look crisp and concise in the final version. If in doubt, throw it out!

Layout

Dense, tightly packed typing is very difficult to read. Therefore spread out your words evenly and neatly on the page to aid the reader.

Use white or very light paper as it will often be photocopied once at the employer's premises and dark colours do not copy well. However, a heavier weight of paper is worth using as it can make your CV stand out from the rest. Buy a box of 100 gram weight paper, perhaps with friends to share the cost.

Keep it simple

I have seen a badly laid out CV in which the author had experimented with many different typefaces or types of print. The result was a complete mishmash of styles and shapes. It put off anyone reading such a confusing document.

Never use more than two different fonts on your CV. More does not mean better-looking. Use different sizes of the same typeface if you want to add some definition for side headings but do not let them dominate the eye at the expense of the important details about you: your name, qualifications and job titles.

Adding emphasis

There are certain features about your CV that you will want to jump out at the reader. The main one is your name. If the employer is sifting through a pile of 20 CVs, you must make sure that yours is easy to spot and remember. If you can use a word processor, put your name in bold or in a slightly larger size font. If the document is typed, underline or double-type it.

Other things to be put in bold, underlined or in some way highlighted are the level of exams you have taken (GCSEs, A levels, etc) and the position of each job that you have held (kitchen porter, journalist, marketing manager, etc). Do not be tempted to highlight the fact that the title of this document is Curriculum Vitae. If the reader cannot tell what the document is, he or she will not be giving it enough attention to act on it anyway. You also do not need to highlight the sub-headings such as 'Name', 'Address', etc through to 'References' either. Your details are what we want to call attention to, and the way to do that is to highlight your achievements in terms of your exams, or courses studied and your job titles.

Look at the examples of CVs in the next chapter to see how impressive this suggested layout looks.

A more creative or varied layout of your CV may possibly be appropriate if you work in a very design-conscious field, but generally I would advise caution. It is better to have a plainer document that is easy to read than a jazzy one that might put people off if they do not share your taste in graphics.

CHAPTER 5

Guidelines and examples

Dos and don'ts

From the information that has been covered so far, there are some general, basic rules to follow when making a good CV for yourself.

Dos

DO   keep it simple – avoid putting the reader off with long words or sentences.

DO   make it clear – all the information should be easy to understand.

DO   keep it short – two pages maximum if possible. If in doubt, throw it out.

DO   be positive – do not elaborate on jobs that you did not make a great success of, or finish; accent instead what you *did* achieve in the situation. For instance, even if you did not gain any exam passes at school or college, still list the subjects that you studied.

DO   assume that the reader does not know what you did in your different jobs; the thing that you think is obvious may not be so to the reader.

DO   take time to put your CV together, and be prepared to make lots of rough notes about your career history first. Chapter 6 takes you through a step-by-step guide to getting started.

DO experiment to see the effect of different aspects of your skills and achievements being highlighted.

DO have two (or more) different versions of your CV if you need to apply for jobs in different career areas – but make sure to note which CV you send off to each employer.

DO get to know your CV inside out – to enable you to talk positively about yourself in an interview.

DO get the finished product word-processed if at all possible.

DO update your CV whenever you have new experiences, qualifications or additional information to include.

Don'ts

DON'T use jargon, or you risk confusing and losing the reader.

DON'T use pretentious language; write as you would speak – simply and clearly.

DON'T copy someone else's CV – it will always look fake.

DON'T invent information – you may well have to prove your knowledge in an interview.

DON'T lie about yourself. You can be dismissed from a job if such misrepresentations are discovered.

DON'T worry about boasting about your strengths – everybody else will be making themselves look extra good too.

DON'T send out the original of your CV if it is difficult for you to get copies. Good photocopies should be used for sending to employers and the original kept clean and safe.

DON'T run out of copies to send out – that will be the time when the job you *really* want comes up.

Examples of CVs

The following pages contain ten examples of CVs for people in different situations. One or more of them may be relevant to you, as you are thinking about what to put in your own CV.

These examples are only included to give you an idea of the many different ways that CVs can be written. Although the names and addresses are fictitious, all the details have been taken from real examples of CVs that have helped people to get the jobs they want.

There is not a CV for every situation, but the examples have been specially picked to represent a wide range of types of CV. Do not copy the information included in the examples, but see if any of them would be an appropriate model for you on which to base your own information.

These are the CVs that are included:

1. School leaver
2. College leaver
3. Graduate (Version 1)
4. Graduate (Version 2)
5. Voluntary work experience
6. Many jobs
7. Gaps between jobs
8. Woman returner
9. Career changer
10. Made redundant.

1. School leaver

CURRICULUM VITAE

NAME: **Moira MAGUIRE**

ADDRESS: 18 Horton Gardens
Nunhead Road
London SE16 1QJ

TELEPHONE: 0171-338 0000

DATE OF BIRTH: 18 August 1983

NATIONALITY: British

EDUCATION:

Sept 1994– July 1999	Stone School London SE16	**Subjects studied:** English, mathematics, science, history, drama

GCSEs:
English	C
Mathematics	C
Science	D

EMPLOYMENT:

June 1997 to date	Azir's Newsagent London SE16	**Sunday papergirl:** sorting out and delivering papers and handling cash

VOLUNTARY WORK:
Since my final year at school I have worked with the elderly
housebound. I regularly visit three people who live locally
and help them with shopping and other household tasks. I
find this work stimulating and rewarding, and intend to con-
tinue with it in my spare time.

OTHER SKILLS:
I was the House Captain in my last year at school and helped
to organised assemblies and sports days. I can type at 45 wpm
and am confident at using a word-processor. I plan to learn to
drive next year.

INTERESTS:
Martial arts, bronze medal for swimming, skateboarding,
cookery and embroidery.

ADDITIONAL INFORMATION:
I am a polite and co-operative person and I apply myself
totally to the task in hand. I am a member of my local youth
group and regularly attend the swimming club. Since the
third year I have been in the school drama group and have
appeared in many productions.

REFERENCES:
Mr Azir (Proprietor)
Azir's Newsagent
218 Watermill Road
London SE16 1HC

Tel: 0171-990 0000

Ms Hardcastle, Head Teacher
Stone School
Lovelace Road
London SE16 3PP

Tel: 0171-731 0000

Moira has no full-time work experience yet, but has managed to get herself a part-time job delivering newspapers. This now provides evidence that she is capable of sticking to a work routine, is trustworthy and determined.

Even without this, she can write about her voluntary experience working with old people while still at school. This implies that she has the ability to get on with a variety of different people, and shows her patience and her concern for others.

Her CV looks very different from most of the others on the following pages because she does not have a list of different jobs that she has done. However, although she has less information than many others, the fact that she has prepared a CV for herself will impress potential employers by setting her apart from other young people of her age.

She has included some interests which make her stand out from other school leavers – martial arts and skateboarding – which also give her topics to discuss at an interview.

Her CV is not much more than her personal details – in fact it could be called a 'Personal Information Sheet' rather than a CV – but it still tells the story of her career to date.

2. College leaver

CURRICULUM VITAE

NAME: **Robin FOSTER**

ADDRESS: 222 Upper Street
                   London N1 5DJ

TELEPHONE: 0171-278 0000

DATE OF BIRTH: 18 June 1978

NATIONALITY: British

MARITAL STATUS: Single

EDUCATION:

1989–1994	Kingsmere Secondary School London E5	**GCSEs:** English C, Maths B, Physics B, Chemistry C, Geography B, Biology B, Sociology B, French E
1994–1996	South West London College London SW15	**A levels:** Maths A, Biology C Physics E
1996–1999	Peele University Peele Northants	**BA Social Science:** Studied economics, history, politics, philosophy, geography and statistics
		Specialised in: Development studies. My thesis was on Third World debt

EMPLOYMENT:

Both my jobs have been part time, and took place during vacations and evenings while at college.

1997	Peele University Union	**Bar Attendant**
1998	Peele University Catering	**Catering Assistant**

OTHER SKILLS:

I can use a computer and am familiar with several word-processing and spreadsheet packages.

INTERESTS:

Keep fit (I was a member of several sports societies while at college), reading, travel, music.

ADDITIONAL INFORMATION:

Having successfully completed my course at Peele University, I am looking to gain employment in an administrative capacity, general office work, or work involving figures. I always contribute fully and would enjoy maintaining high standards of accuracy and attention to detail. I am keen to start my career and would be a loyal and dependable employee.

REFERENCES:

Professor S Welt
Peele University
Peele
Northants NT5 5BG

Tel: 01772 00000

Dr L M Cash
97 The Crescent
London W5 2PB

Tel: 0181-435 0000

Robin has made the most of the space available to him to give full information about his college career. He has given detailed information about his course at college and about the jobs he did while studying. Without any full-time work experience, he needs to bring out any other factors which may help to persuade a future employer that he is worth taking on.

He mentions his active involvement in sport to show that he has a variety of interests. He also uses the 'Additional information' section as a chance to sell himself to the employer. He stresses his good points to show the contribution he could make.

3. Graduate (Version 1)

CURRICULUM VITAE

NAME:	**Michael SMITH**
ADDRESS:	935 Main Road Manchester M16 8AP
TELEPHONE:	0161-693 0000
DATE OF BIRTH:	27 August 1974
MARITAL STATUS:	Married

EDUCATION:

1981– 1992	Frankwell Secondary School Shrewsbury Shropshire	**GCSEs:** Seven subjects including English Language, Literature and Mathematics
		A levels: Mathematics B, Geography C
1992– 1995	Lowston Polytechnic Lowston Surrey	**BA (Hons) Business Studies:** Specialised in marketing and financial management
1998– 1999	London Massage School London SW18	**ITEC Course in Massage, Anatomy and Physiology:** Training in techniques to give professional, therapeutic treatment, allied with a sound knowledge of the systems of the body and their relevance to massage
1999– date	London Massage School London SW18	**Intermediate Massage Training Course:** Continued training by studying shiatsu, medical massage, reflexology and breathing and relaxation techniques

EMPLOYMENT:

| 1997–1999 | Private work in the London area | **Consultant Masseur:** Relaxing, professional therapeutic massage with essential oils |
| 1995–1997 | Employment agencies in the London area | **Various clerical positions:** General office work and dealing with the public |

OTHER SKILLS:
I have a working knowledge of aromatherapy, reflexology and shiatsu. I have a current, clean driving licence and have recently acquired basic keyboard skills.

ADDITIONAL INFORMATION:
I have always used my hands in a creative way, and found massage a natural progression, which is immensely rewarding and fulfilling.

I am a friendly, outgoing person, and am able to get on with people in all situations. I am reliable, trustworthy, punctual and meticulous. I have the ability to work well as part of a team, can deal competently with administrative duties and particularly enjoyed the financial aspects of my business course.

REFEREES:
Bernadette Beckett (Principal)
London Massage School
Westcliffe Road
London SW18 2HB

Tel: 0181-339 0000

Clare Maledy (Course Tutor)
BA Business Studies
Lowston Polytechnic
Lee Street
Lowston
Surrey KT3 2MN

Tel: 0181-448 0000

Michael is trying to use his massage qualification to get a job in a health or sports centre. However, his background is in business studies, so he uses the 'Additional Information' section of his CV to explain his interest in massage.

He gives most details about his interest in massage, the subjects that he studied in his practical training and the fact that he has spent a period self-employed as a masseur.

He is still considering a career in business, so he has created another CV, to apply for a different type of work.

4. Graduate (Version 2)

CURRICULUM VITAE

NAME:	**Michael SMITH**
ADDRESS:	935 Main Road
	Manchester M16 8AP
TELEPHONE:	0161-693 0000
DATE OF BIRTH:	27 August 1974
MARITAL STATUS:	Married

EDUCATION:

1981–1992	Frankwell Secondary School Shrewsbury Shropshire	**GCSEs:** Seven subjects including English Language, Literature and Mathematics **A levels:** Mathematics B, Geography C
1992–1995	Lowston Polytechnic Lowston Surrey	**BA (Hons) Business Studies:** Specialised in marketing and financial management, completed thesis on European business training
1998–1999	London Massage School London SW18	**ITEC Course in Massage, Anatomy and Physiology:** Training in techniques to give all types of massage, currently studying at intermediate level

EMPLOYMENT:

1997–1999	Self-employed in the London area	**Consultant Masseur:** Relaxing, professional therapeutic massage with essential oils
1995–1997	Employment agencies in the London area	**Various clerical positions:** Dealing with the public and filing, answering phone calls, writing letters, typing, keeping petty cash account

OTHER SKILLS:

I am a keen masseur, and have a working knowledge of aromatherapy, reflexology and shiatsu. I have a current, clean driving licence and have recently acquired basic keyboard skills.

ADDITIONAL INFORMATION:

I enjoyed my degree course which introduced me to the business world. I specialised in financial analysis and the marketing function, and completed my thesis on the different types of business trading across Europe.

I am a friendly, outgoing person, and am able to get on with people in all situations. I am reliable, trustworthy, punctual and meticulous. I have the ability to work well as part of a team, can deal competently with administrative duties and am keen to establish my career in a clerical or administrative capacity.

REFEREES:

Clare Maledy (Course Tutor)
BA Business Studies
Lowston Polytechnic
Lee Street
Lowston
Surrey KT3 2MN

Tel: 0181-448 0000

Bernadette Beckett (Principal)
London Massage School
Westcliffe Road
London SW18 2HB

Tel: 0181-339 0000

It would be difficult for Michael to have just one CV which detailed all the information that he needs to apply for both the types of work that he is interested in.

His second CV has the same basic information about his personal details, qualifications and experience, but stresses his interest in a career in administration instead of massage. He includes more information about his college course, his office experience and changes the 'Additional Information' section to appeal more to employers of clerical staff.

These two CVs, sent out with care to appropriate employers, will enhance his chances of gaining one of the types of employment of his choice.

5. Voluntary experience

CURRICULUM VITAE

NAME:	**Geraldine CLARKE**

ADDRESS:
99 Eugenia House
Norton Street
Chipping Campden
Gloucestershire
GL2 1KK

TELEPHONE:	016732 0000
DATE OF BIRTH:	14 April 1972
NATIONALITY:	British
MARITAL STATUS:	Single

EDUCATION:

1986–1989	Josiah Wedgwood School London NE21	**GCSEs:** English, Maths, French, Technical Drawing and Art
1989–1993	North London Technical College London NE17	**BTEC National Diploma:** Visual research, objective drawing, furniture design, drawing office practice, foundation science, industrial organisation
		BTEC Higher National Diploma: Antique history and restoration specialising in gilding and Victoriana

VOLUNTARY EXPERIENCE:

1993–1999	Green World Bath Avon	**Membership Secretary:** Dealing with all letter and phone enquiries, setting up new computer system and helping to train paid staff

HOBBIES AND INTERESTS:

I enjoy photography, reading, windsurfing, sailing, skiing and going to the cinema and theatre.

ADDITIONAL INFORMATION:

Since leaving college, I have been looking after a sick relative. I used my two free days each week to volunteer for a local charity. During the last six years I have become very involved in their business, and have recently been part of a team which designed and established a new computerised membership system.

Although this work was unpaid, the skills I have gained are those used in any business environment, such as being part of a team, keeping to deadlines, working under pressure and delegating tasks.

I am now keen to start applying these skills in an organisation, where I can make a full contribution.

REFERENCES:

Mr M Baldock (Director)
Green World
Hunerk House
99 North Street
Bath
Avon
BR4 2JK

Tel: 01382 000000

Mr J Phillips
BTEC Graphic Design Course Director
North London Technical College
Swift Road
London NE178 3PU

Tel: 0181-830 0000

Geraldine has only ever done voluntary work, but she uses the 'Additional Information' section to explain why. She had sensibly chosen voluntary work in the field in which she wanted to work, so is able to stress what useful experience she has gained.

Her years of volunteering have also gained her a glowing reference from the director of the charity concerned.

6. Many jobs

CURRICULUM VITAE

NAME:	**Adam PETERS**
ADDRESS:	3 Upland Street London SE21 1ST
TELEPHONE:	0181-946 0000
DATE OF BIRTH:	19 March 1972
NATIONALITY:	British
MARITAL STATUS:	Single

EDUCATION:

Sept 1983– May 1988	Greens' School London SE3 1JK	**Subjects studied:** English, maths, science, art, metalwork, woodwork
Sept 1988– July 1989	Central College London SW1 3KA	**Which Job? Course**

EMPLOYMENT:

Aug 1997– Mar 1999	Freshfood Dairies London SW16	**Milk-roundsman:** Bookkeeping, dealing with the public, handling cash, ordering stock, banking and deliveries
Sept 1996– Apr 1997	True Personnel London E16 1HH	**Recruitment consultant:** Recruitment advertising, interviewing, wages, canvassing for new business, general office duties
July 1994– Aug 1996	Bales' Business Services London SE17 1JD	**Warehouseman:** Storing valuable data files, keeping accurate records, dealing with clients

Mar 1989– July 1994	Various temporary agencies around London, working as a general assistant and in manual work	
Aug 1987– Mar 1989	Jay's Stores London SE6 3RT	**Cashier:** Shelf-filling, responsible for cash, checking all deliveries, ordering shop stock

INTERESTS:

Squash, snooker, swimming, bowling, crosswords, collecting stamps, walking my dog.

ADDITIONAL INFORMATION:

I am always keen to take on extra responsibility at work. I am trustworthy and hard-working and have often worked overtime in my previous jobs.

I would like to work in a position which involves contact with the public, as I get on well with a wide variety of people. I enjoy being part of a team, but can also work alone and unsupervised.

REFERENCES

Mr Hugh MacKinnon
(Foreman at Bales' Business Services)
14 Beach House
Brighton Road
London SE21 1HF

Tel: (work) 0171-493 0000

Mr Adrian Smithson
(Accountant)
134 Eugenia Road
London SW4 4TL

Tel: (work) 0181-699 0000

Adam has plenty of jobs listed on his CV already. He has grouped together some of his work experience, between 1989 and 1994, to cut further jobs out. Those that he is omitting only duplicate the jobs that he has listed in full elsewhere.

He gives full details of some jobs to show the skills that he has learned, grouping others together instead of listing them all.

7. Gaps between jobs

CURRICULUM VITAE

NAME: **Shola ODUNTAN**

ADDRESS: 25b Aubert Road
Birmingham B15 1NS

TELEPHONE: 0121-661 0000

E-MAIL ADDRESS: s.oduntan@corfield.com

DATE OF BIRTH: 2 February 1964

NATIONALITY: Nigerian (with full British Citizenship)

MARITAL STATUS: Married

HEALTH: Excellent

EDUCATION:

| 1975–1981 | Government College Lagos Nigeria | **O levels:** 5 subjects including English |
| 1981–1983 | Bournebrook College Birmingham B29 | **Course in Business Studies** |

EMPLOYMENT:

| 1993–1997 | Njoku Industries Birmingham B3 | **Marketing Assistant:** Responsible for all the marketing support activity for the company, producing and administering direct mail campaigns, creating and maintaining databases, planning, designing and implementing advertising, organising exhibitions, setting market budgets |

| 1987–1991 | Gold and Sons Birmingham B12 | **Advertisement Production Manager:** Organising plans and advert layouts, liaising with clients and advertising agents, designers, printers, proofreading and passing pages for filming and setting deadlines for the sections |

ADDITIONAL INFORMATION:
In the late 1970s I travelled extensively in Africa with a relative, supporting myself through trading activities. In 1991/2 I toured Europe, doing temporary, seasonal work. These periods of travelling have given me the opportunity to learn a great deal about other countries and cultures, and I have seen many different ways of organising businesses and society in general.

OTHER SKILLS:
During the last year, I have used a local resource centre to learn keyboarding and computer skills and am now able to use QuarkXpress, a desk-top publishing package. I can speak four different African languages and basic French.

INTERESTS:
Reading, listening to music, gardening, yoga and aerobics, writing short stories.

REFERENCES:
Mrs A Collins
Personnel Director
Njoku Industries
Wyndham Industrial Estate
Mill Lane
Birmingham B3 2DD
Tel: 0121-572 0000

Mr O Burkitt
Director, Gold and Sons
25 Field Lane
Birmingham B12 6LQ
Tel: 0121-283 0000

In order to explain the fact that she has had long gaps in her career history, Shola gives details about the periods that she spent travelling. She stresses the benefits that these periods have given her and shows how she has developed as a person.

8. Woman returner

CURRICULUM VITAE

NAME:	**Barbara ANDERSON**
ADDRESS:	9 Redlands Tower
	Culvert Road
	Sidcup
	Kent
	DA15 3TT
TELEPHONE:	0181-300 0000
DATE OF BIRTH:	10 December 1971
NATIONALITY:	British
MARITAL STATUS:	Married

EDUCATION:

1982–	Sacred Heart Grammar	**GCSEs:**
1988	School	5 subjects
	Sidcup	including English
	Kent	
1988–	Sidcup Technical College	**A levels:**
1989	Sidcup	English C,
	Kent	History C

EMPLOYMENT:

Sept 1989–	Department of Employment	**Executive Officer:**
June 1993	Unemployment Benefit	Supervising staff,
	Office	organising work,
	Mottingham	dealing with the
	Kent	public, sorting out
		computer problems

OTHER SKILLS:

I am able to use computers and have recently learnt word-processing in my spare time.

INTERESTS:

I enjoy reading historical novels and biographies, going to the cinema and joining in outdoor activities with my children.

ADDITIONAL INFORMATION:

I was a prefect at school. In June 1993, I left the Civil Service to bring up my two young children. As a full-time mother since that date, I have acquired new skills, such as the ability to organise and communicate on different levels, to use my imagination, and to be patient and flexible.

REFERENCES:

Ms Irene Hill
22 Stafford Road
High Wycombe
Buckinghamshire
HW1 1LD

Tel: 01291 00000

Father Paul Behan
Parish Priest
Church of Our Lady
Crimscott Lane
London WC2B 1YB

Tel: 0171-832 0000

Barbara is anxious to get back to work after bringing up her young children. She sensibly stresses the skills that she has acquired during her time in the home and emphasises how keen she is to re-establish her career.

She gives full details of her previous job and shows that she has many interests.

9. Career changer

CURRICULUM VITAE

NAME:	**Marilyn BROWNE**
ADDRESS:	806 Tiverton Place London N5 2HX
TELEPHONE:	O181-928 0000
DATE OF BIRTH:	20 May 1966
MARITAL STATUS:	Divorced
NATIONALITY:	British
HEALTH:	Excellent

EDUCATION:

1979–1984	Ragdale School Birmingham B14 1LJ	**O levels:** English A, Biology B, Maths B, History C, Chemistry B
1984–1986	Charing Court Hospital London W5 2JN	**Pupil Nurse for State Enrolled Nurse**

EMPLOYMENT:

Nov 1993–Jan 1999	Queen's Hospital London SE3 2HJ	**State Enrolled Nurse:** Working in theatre with the Sister, making sure theatre list is correctly written, that theatre is ready for use, instruments are correct for different operations, teaching student nurses, completing appropriate paperwork, liaising between hospital departments, taking phone calls

June 1990– Aug 1993	Waterside Hospital London W1 3PP	**State Enrolled Nurse:** Looking after medical and surgical patients, doing ward rounds with doctors, making sure that patients' notes were up to date, transferring patients to theatre, dealing with enquiries, dispensing drugs
Nov 1986– May 1990	Charing Court Hospital London W5 2JN	**State Enrolled Nurse:** Working in out-patients department, making sure patients' notes were completed, getting doctors' trays ready for examination, answering phone calls, dealing with patients and medical sales representatives

INTERESTS:

Horse-riding, badminton, walking my dog, learning keyboard skills, reading nursing journals.

ADDITIONAL INFORMATION:

My working life to date has been mainly caring for people. This has made me patient and tolerant when dealing with the public. In hospital, patients and their relatives are often scared and distressed, even angry, and they need calm but firm handling.

As a result of my State Enrolled Nurse training, I am familiar with the study of biology, chemistry and drugs, and have had 13 years' experience as a qualified nurse working in a variety of different medical establishments.

I now wish to use my professional skills in combination with my main interest, which is caring for animals. I feel my nursing skills together with my trustworthy, hard-working and dedicated character, would make me ideally suited to a career as an animal nurse.

REFERENCES

Mr Simon Howarth (Theatre Manager)
Queen's Hospital
London SE3 2HJ
Tel: 0171-339 0000

Mrs J Michaels
21 Green Vale
London SE16 2KY
Tel: 0171-231 0000

Marilyn wants to change her career after nearly 15 years in nursing. Although her experience will be very appropriate for her desired career in animal nursing, she needs to justify her decision to change her plans.

By using the 'Additional Information' section to explain her ideas, she can answer the questions which any future employer may have.

10. Made redundant

CURRICULUM VITAE

NAME:	**Melanie RANDALL**
ADDRESS:	5 Somerfield Street London SW9 4LH
TELEPHONE:	0171-889 0000
DATE OF BIRTH:	23 September 1972
NATIONALITY:	British
MARITAL STATUS:	Divorced

EDUCATION:

1983– 1988	Trinity School London SE8	**GCSEs:** English, Mathematics, Art, Geography, Domestic Science

EMPLOYMENT:

1996– 1998	Popular Pizzas London EC2	**Senior Assistant:** In charge of seven staff, organising work rotas, ordering stock, cashing-up, recruitment and training of staff, dealing with sales representatives
1993– 1986	Popular Pizzas London EC2	**Catering Assistant:** Helping to prepare fast food, general kitchen work, waiting at table and handling cash

| 1990–1992 | Newgate Inn London E3 | **Kitchen Supervisor:** In charge of busy kitchen, menu planning, cooking, cleaning, stock control, bookkeeping, banking and staff supervision |
| 1988–1990 | Newgate Inn London E3 | **Kitchen Assistant:** Helping out with serving, preparing food, and running special events |

INTERESTS:
Listening to music, reading, cooking and entertaining, and playing pool and darts. I arrange Charity Darts and Pool matches for the Multiple Sclerosis Society.

ADDITIONAL INFORMATION:
I am punctual, reliable and able to work enthusiastically under pressure, either within a team or alone. I am straightforward, positive and a fair person with a friendly disposition and a good sense of humour. This has aided me in the supervision of staff and in extensive dealings with clients and the public.

I have been in positions of trust, handling money on behalf of others. I have high moral standards and am well-balanced and controlled. My aim is to find employment in an environment with high standards and productivity.

REFERENCES:
Dick Nye
Manager
The Newgate Inn
Newgate Street
London E3 3FG
Tel: 0171-447 0000

Desmond Cook
Area Manager
Popular Pizzas
New Road
London EC2 3LR
Tel: 0171-831 0000

Melanie had the misfortune to be made redundant, not once but twice, from her jobs in the catering trade. The first time it happened she had to start in a more lowly position and work her way back up again to a more responsible position – and now she has to begin again.

It is more difficult to find employment once you are unemployed, so she has filled the 'Additional Information' section with as much positive information about herself as possible. The 'Interests' section shows the charity fund-raising work that she is involved in, all of which adds to the impression that she has a lot to offer.

CHAPTER 6

Preparing your own CV

Step-by-step guide

To recap on the main points made in this book, here is a step-by-step guide to preparing your own CV.

Step 1: The draft CV

Choose a quiet time when you will not be disturbed, as you will need all your concentration for the task.

Using the blank form at the end of this chapter on pages 81–82, start to fill in all the sections, beginning with the personal details through to your referees. Refer to Chapter 3 to help you to complete each section.

Education

Do not hold back at this stage. Starting from secondary school, put down every school and college, course and qualification that you have ever attended, studied or gained.

Employment

Follow this by noting down every employer that you have ever worked for, whether it be full time, part time, holiday or voluntary work. This is your raw material from which will come the finished version of your CV. You will not want to include all these details in the real thing, but writing them down in rough will help you to decide what to use later on. Try and be as accurate as possible within relevant dates.

Other skills
Rack your brains for things to add to this section. Driving licence, first aid, computer and word-processing skills would all fit in here. There may be some particular skills that are relevant to the job you are applying for that you have not been able to include elsewhere, such as using certain tools, machinery or equipment. Language ability should be mentioned in this part of the document.

Interests
For this draft CV, include any pastimes or hobbies that you have ever spent time on, to give you a list from which to choose three or four sporty pursuits; then write down the same number of activities which show your other interests.

Additional information
This is the section where you can really go to town. If you want your CV to jump out at an employer, use this space to pick out your particular strengths. Just write down what your best friend, or perhaps your mother, would say about you – on a good day! How would they describe your best points to an employer?

Don't worry about sounding boastful. This is the only information that employers will have to go on, so this section is telling them that they should definitely invite you for an interview.

References
Check with both your referees that they are quite happy to be included in your CV. Make sure that their details are correct.

Step 2: Editing your CV
Now read everything you have written down so far and decide what to include or delete. You will need to spend the most time on the 'Education' and 'Employment' sections. The rule here is – if in doubt, leave it out, so the only information that remains is clear, concise and interesting to read. It must

tell the story of your career to date, stressing your achievements and showing your development.

Look through the examples in Chapter 5 to see the sort of information that other people have included in their CVs. Look at each section of your draft document and try to think what needs to be included to give a fair picture of your experience. This step can only be done by you, but remember that the whole CV should only cover two sheets of A4 paper; you will not have room for anything but the essential information. Ask yourself 'Does this part of the CV add to the total impression?' before you leave it in.

At this stage, enlist a friend or relative to take an objective look at what you have written. They may be able to tell you if some information needs to made clearer, or if some parts of the CV are too long or too short. They may also be able to spot mistakes that you have completely ignored.

Step 3: The final version

Now check through everything you have written. If you are sure it is all correct and accurate, then you are ready to get the final version typed up.

However good the person is who types up your CV, you must make sure that you check and re-check the document for accuracy of content and attractive presentation. If your CV is produced on a word-processor, it will be a fairly simple matter to make corrections; time spent proof-reading at this stage will save having to hurry later on.

Once the document has been typed up, show it to somebody else. Another person will often be able to spot errors that you will miss, however many times you reread it.

If you now feel happy that your CV is a good representation of your strengths and assets, the real test is to use it to apply for jobs and to contact employers.

Step 4: The covering letter

You will never send out your CV on its own. At the very least, you will write a letter to the employer saying which job you are applying for. Even if a covering letter has not specifically been requested, you can use the opportunity to explain more about yourself.

What goes in a covering letter?

In most cases you will need to say why you are sending your CV, a little about yourself and what you want to happen next. A letter one to two pages in length can reiterate what you have to offer an employer. Go back to the list of your best qualities that you used for the 'Additional Information' section and restate the key points in a different form in the letter.

Obviously, all letters will be personal to the writer, but here are some general hints about the way to put your covering letter together, followed by an example:

- Keep the letter as brief as possible – the employer has already got two pages of your CV to read. It should never be longer than two sides of A4 paper.

- This is your introduction to your CV – make sure your letter is interesting enough for your CV to be actually read. Think of this letter as a sales document. Use short sentences and positive words to create a memorable and attractive impression.

- Always be very courteous – it costs you nothing and politeness cannot help but impress the reader.

- Use new, unlined paper to create a good impression. The covering letter can be word-processed or typed. Handwriting is much more unusual these days. If it must be handwritten ensure it is *extremely* neat. Use the same type of paper as you did for the CV if possible, so they match.

- Take as much care over the letter as you have with your CV. Your hard work on the CV may be wasted if the employer takes a dislike to a messy letter, and throws the lot into the waste-paper bin.

- If you are sending your CV in response to an advertise-ment, make sure that you address the letter to the correct person, and say where you saw the vacancy. The company may be advertising several jobs at the same time, in differ-ent publications, and will need to know which one you are applying for.

- If you are approaching employers who may have vacan-cies, but who have not yet advertised, try to find out the name of the person you want to approach and address the letter to him or her personally.

- Shrug off the worry that your letter sounds boastful. It needs to be larger than life to get you noticed.

- Make a list of all the places to which you send your CV, and the dates it was sent. If you do not hear anything, it is always worth ringing the company in three or four weeks' time, just to check if there is any news.

- Attach the letter to your CV with a paperclip so it does not get separated.

Example of a covering letter

Dear Ms Charnley

I enclose my curriculum vitae for your attention. I am a 31 year-old mother of two children. As you can see from my CV, I have five years' experience of clerical work in a busy office and have recently completed a word-processing course at a local training centre.

I thoroughly enjoy working in administration and I know that unless the paperwork is accurate any company will suffer. Therefore I am careful about checking my work and always help my colleagues out to get the work done.

I am highly motivated, ambitious and enjoy working to deadlines. I have excellent references and would relish the chance to work as part of the team at White Brothers.

I should be grateful if you would contact me if you have any vacancies in your company, or keep my information on file in case of future openings.

Thank you for your attention in this matter. I look forward to hearing from you.

Yours sincerely

Helen Guyer

Blank CV

CURRICULUM VITAE

NAME:

ADDRESS:

TELEPHONE NUMBER:

DATE OF BIRTH:

NATIONALITY:

MARITAL STATUS:

EDUCATION:

(Dates)   (Name and location)   (Qualifications or subjects studied)

EMPLOYMENT:

(Dates)   (Name and location)   (Position held and main duties)

OTHER SKILLS:

INTERESTS:

ADDITIONAL INFORMATION:

REFERENCES:

Other sources of help

The Careers Service
In some areas of the country, the staff in your local careers service can offer help and advice to adults. They will have reference books about employers and applying for jobs, and understanding, skilled staff who can help you put your CV together if you get stuck. Find the telephone number in the local phone book and ring them to find out more.

Employment Agencies
Agencies may wish to compile a CV for you for a particular type of job to help them to 'sell' you to an employer. They charge the employer if you are placed with a company and you will not always be allowed to have a copy of the CV they compile for your own use.

Private Careers Counsellors
You can get help from careers counsellors who work privately and who make a charge for their service. This can be very expensive and although they will help you to put the CV together and then print it out on a top quality printer, you will also be charged extra for any reprints and amendments that you may require in the future.

Learning Direct
The Learning Direct number, 0800 100 900, is a Government funded telephone help line available to everyone. Ring the freephone number and you will be given advice about local sources of help on careers and learning issues. This could include where to contact the types of organisations mentioned above.

TEC/LEC
Your local Training and Enterprise Council, (Local Enterprise Company in Scotland) may be able to put you in touch with local training organisations who can help you with your CV. Their number will be in the phone book.

Further reading from Kogan Page

Career, Aptitude and Selection Tests, Jim Barrett, 1998

From CV to Shortlist: Job hunting for professionals, Tony Vickers, 1997

Get the Job You Want in 30 Days!, Gary Joseph Grappo, 1998

Great Answers to Tough Interview Questions, Martin John Yate, 4th edition, 1998

How to Master Personality Questionnaires, Mark Parkinson, 1997

How to Master Psychometric Tests, Mark Parkinson, 1997

How to Pass Selection Tests, Mike Bryant and Sanjay Modha, 2nd edition, 1998

How You Can Get That Job! Application forms and letters made easy, Rebecca Corfield, 2nd edition, 1999

Marketing Yourself and Your Career, Jane Ballback and Jan Slater, 1998

Net that Job! Using the World Wide Web to develop your career and find work, Irene Krechowiecka, 1998

Rate Yourself! Assess your skills, personality and abilities for the job you want, Marthe Sansregret and Dyane Adams, 1998

Readymade CVs: A source book for job hunters, Lynn Williams, 1996

Readymade Interview Questions, Malcolm Peel, 2nd edition, 1996

Readymade Job Search Letters, Lynn Williams, 1995

Successful Interview Skills, Rebecca Corfield, 2nd edition, 1999

Test Your Own Aptitude, Jim Barrett and Geoff Williams, 2nd edition, 1990

The A–Z of Careers and Jobs, edited by Diane Burston, 8th edition, 1997

30 Minutes Before Your Job Interview, June Lines, 1997

30 Minutes to Prepare a Job Application, June Lines, 1997
Unlocking Your Career Potential, Jane Ballback and Jan Slater, 1998

Kogan Page Careers Series

These practical guides range from *Careers in Accountancy* to *Careers in the Theatre.* They are packed with useful information. School and college leavers, graduates and anyone considering a career change will find the books an invaluable source of information and help in planning their future careers. All titles contain details of:

- careers openings and prospects
- educational requirements and training opportunities
- how to apply for jobs
- likely working conditions
- university and college courses.

Kogan Page books are available from good bookshops. In case of difficulty, contact the publisher at 120 Pentonville Road, London N1 9JN; 0171 278 0433 (24-hour answering service).

Index